VITAL TO EARTH!
Keystone Species Explained

T0012410

MANGROVE TREES
IN THEIR ECOSYSTEMS

by Olivia Hammond

BEARPORT
PUBLISHING

Minneapolis, Minnesota

Credits
Cover and title page, © Marie Hickman/Getty; 4–5, © Paul Kingsley/Alamy; 6–7, © Prantik Chatterjee
/500px/Getty; 8, © ENVIROSENSE/Shutterstock; 9, © apomares/iStock; 10–11, © Ethan Daniels/
Shutterstock; 12–13, © Fahroni/Alamy; 14–15, © Damsea/Shutterstock; 15, © Damsea/Shutterstock; 17,
© xeni4ka/iStock; 18–19, © Panther Media GmbH/Alamy; 20–21, © R. Gino Santa Maria/Adobe Stock;
22–23, © James Caldwell/Alamy; 24–25, © Arun Roisri/Getty; 26–27, © Dragonite__East/iStock; 28,
© Damocean/iStock; 29T, © LSOphoto/iStock; 29TM, © Imgorthand/iStock; 29M, © LeManna/iStock;
29BM, © PeopleImages/iStock; 29B, © jacoblund/iStock.

Bearport Publishing Company Product Development Team
President: Jen Jenson; Director of Product Development: Spencer Brinker; Managing Editor: Allison Juda;
Associate Editor: Naomi Reich; Associate Editor: Tiana Tran; Art Director: Colin O'Dea; Designer: Elena
Klinkner; Designer: Kayla Eggert; Product Development Assistant: Owen Hamlin

STATEMENT ON USAGE OF GENERATIVE ARTIFICIAL INTELLIGENCE
Bearport Publishing remains committed to publishing high-quality nonfiction books. Therefore, we
restrict the use of generative AI to ensure accuracy of all text and visual components pertaining to a
book's subject. See BearportPublishing.com for details.

Library of Congress Cataloging-in-Publication Data is available at www.loc.gov or upon request from the
publisher.

ISBN: 979-8-88916-630-6 (hardcover)
ISBN: 979-8-88916-637-5 (paperback)
ISBN: 979-8-88916-643-6 (ebook)

Copyright © 2024 Bearport Publishing Company. All rights reserved. No part of this publication may
be reproduced in whole or in part, stored in any retrieval system, or transmitted in any form or by any
means, electronic, mechanical, photocopying, recording, or otherwise, without written permission from
the publisher.

For more information, write to Bearport Publishing, 5357 Penn Avenue South, Minneapolis, MN 55419.

Contents

The Tree of Life

A lush forest growing from the salty water along the coast is full of life. Small fish swim among the tangle of twisted tree roots. Snails crawl on the sturdy roots in the still water. Crabs and insects munch on the plants' green leaves, while birds, monkeys, and even sloths make themselves at home in the branches.

What are the strange plants at the center of all this activity? They are mangrove trees, and they are vital to their **ecosystems**.

There are about 80 different **species** of mangroves, all of which grow as either shrubs or trees. The plants form forests in salty marshes, along muddy coastlines, and in tidal **estuaries**.

Some kinds of mangroves stand tall on stilt-like roots that shoot above the water. These are called prop roots.

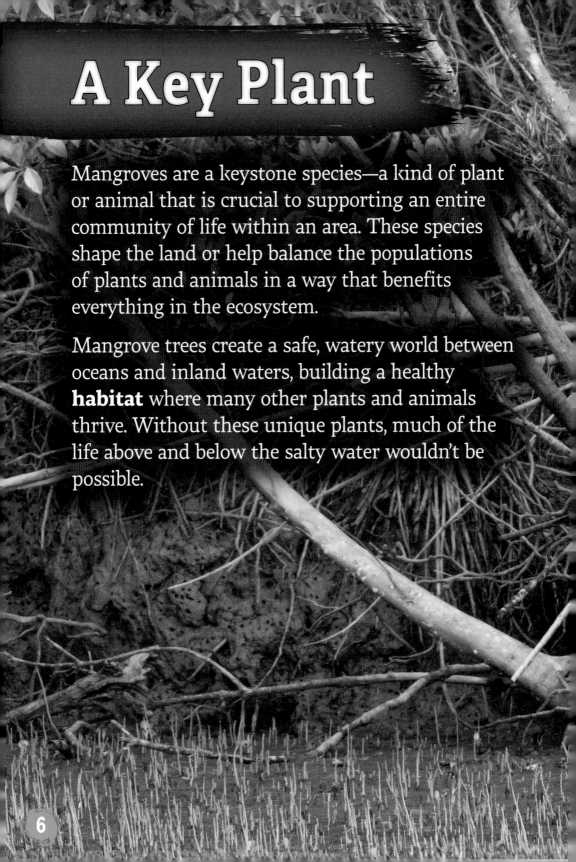

A Key Plant

Mangroves are a keystone species—a kind of plant or animal that is crucial to supporting an entire community of life within an area. These species shape the land or help balance the populations of plants and animals in a way that benefits everything in the ecosystem.

Mangrove trees create a safe, watery world between oceans and inland waters, building a healthy **habitat** where many other plants and animals thrive. Without these unique plants, much of the life above and below the salty water wouldn't be possible.

More than 1,500 plant and animal species depend on mangroves. This includes fish and seabirds as well as mammals, such as monkeys, sloths, and even tigers.

Salt Survivors

Mangroves grow in conditions that would kill most other plants. They have adapted to take in water but keep things from getting too salty. Some have roots that **filter** out salt as water passes through. Other mangroves let out salt through special **glands** in their leaves.

All the salt in the water also leads to low levels of oxygen in the soil. So, mangroves have roots that rise feet above the water. These roots pull the oxygen they need from the air around them rather than from the oxygen-poor soil below.

Salt on mangrove leaves

Plants need water to help them make food through photosynthesis. Oxygen helps plants turn this food into the energy they need to live and grow.

Roots to the Rescue!

Below the waves, the mangroves' unique roots work to shape the habitat. The trees grow out of the water along the coast, providing a barrier between the open ocean and inland waterways. The dense cluster of mangrove roots slows large waves that come crashing toward the forests from the ocean. **Sediment** moves toward land in these waves, but it settles to the ocean floor as the roots slow the water. The tangle of roots then holds the sediment in place, preventing it from pushing farther inland. In turn, all the sediment also holds the mangroves and other plants securely in the soil.

Sediment caught by mangrove roots is turned into a thick, rich soil called peat. **Nutrients** in the peat feed sea life, including shrimp, crabs, and fish.

Standing Up to the Storm

Because of how closely together they grow, these trees can even tame the power of strong storms that would otherwise destroy coastal habitats. When powerful, storm-driven ocean water crashes into mangrove forests, the dense structure slows the waves. It lessens the energy of the impact by spreading it out around the roots. It also makes it harder for ocean water to surge onto land, protecting not only life in the mangrove forests but also plants and animals farther inland.

Above the water's surface, storm winds run up against mangrove trunks, branches, and leaves. The winds then lose force and speed, causing less damage to the areas within and beyond the forests.

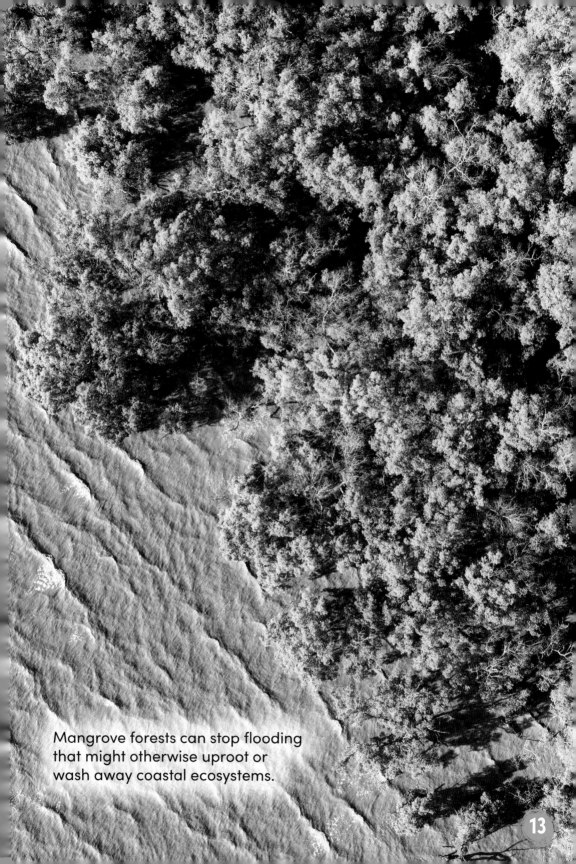

Mangrove forests can stop flooding that might otherwise uproot or wash away coastal ecosystems.

A Mangrove Home

Many living things find safety in the sturdy ecosystems kept in place by mangrove forests. The still waters are gentle enough for smaller animals not ready for the wild ocean waves. Sponges, oysters, snails, and worms cling to mangrove roots to keep from drifting into the dangerous open ocean. Crabs and shrimp hide in the soft mud beneath the trees.

The tangled roots also provide lots of hiding places from larger **predators**. Many kinds of fish and shellfish gather in the shelter of the roots to make babies, raise their young, and keep them from harm.

Some creatures live in the branches and aboveground roots of the mangrove forest. Most of the endangered pygmy three-toed sloths left in the wild live in mangrove trees off the coast of Panama.

Welcome to the Feast

Busy mangrove forests also form the foundation of coastal food webs. Birds, bats, bees, and butterflies feed on mangrove flowers. Crabs, caterpillars, spiders, and ants chew on their leaves.

When the leaves fall off mangroves and begin to break down in the water, their nutrients feed tiny creatures, such as **algae** and plankton. These are then slurped up by crabs, shrimp, jellyfish, and small fish. Then, larger fish and other meat-eaters gobble up the smaller creatures of this watery forest.

Above the waterline, ants, moths, termites, and mosquitoes crawl along the trees' bark. They attract hungry insect eaters, such as monkeys, sloths, lizards, and frogs.

Keeping Water Clean

In addition to providing food and shelter, mangroves keep things clean. The incredible plants filter **pollutants** from the water.

Without mangroves cleaning the water, the underwater ecosystem is in danger of tipping out of balance. Algae often feed on pollutants. When there is too much food for these tiny living things, they begin to grow out of control. Algal blooms—thick growths of the slimy stuff—block sunlight, remove oxygen from the water, and release **toxins**. This kills many animals and plants.

Rainstorms often wash fuel from roads, wastewater from sewers, and chemicals from farms into waterways. Once in the water, these pollutants can be hard to remove.

Algal blooms often coat
the water in green growth.

Beating the Heat

Even life far from the coasts benefits from the cleaning powers of mangroves. We burn **fossil fuels** to power our cars, homes, and businesses. Every time we do, we release a gas called **carbon dioxide** that traps heat around Earth and causes temperatures to rise. This extra warmth is changing our **climate** and causing unusual weather, monster storms, and severe droughts.

Mangroves pull carbon from the air and use it to build roots, branches, and leaves. When the leaves fall and the trees die, they sink to the seafloor. All the heat-trapping carbon they contain is buried there, where it can do no harm.

Sea levels are rising due to the warming planet, putting mangroves at risk. They cannot stay above rising tides in some places. If their roots are completely covered in water, the plants will drown.

We Need These Trees

In addition to their positive environmental impact, mangroves are helpful to humans in other ways. People use the plants' wood to build houses, boats, and fishing poles. Mangrove materials can also be used to make soaps, perfumes, insecticides, and many kinds of medicine.

Some people get honey from bees that make their homes in mangrove forests. Others make a living off fishing among the trees. In the Gulf of California in Mexico, about 23 percent of fish are caught in mangrove habitats.

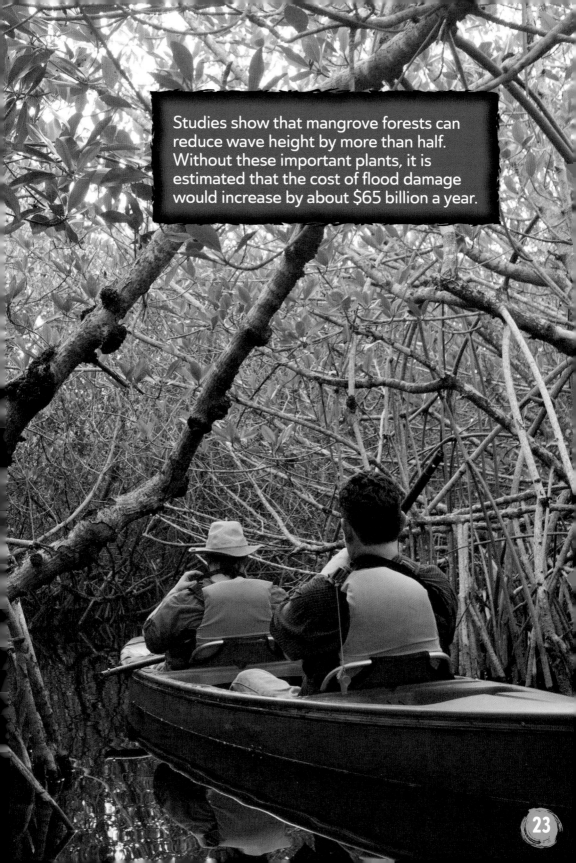

Studies show that mangrove forests can reduce wave height by more than half. Without these important plants, it is estimated that the cost of flood damage would increase by about $65 billion a year.

Missing Mangroves

Given how important mangrove forests are, you would think we would be doing everything possible to protect them. But the trees are disappearing fast. Humans have torn down many forests to make way to build homes and businesses along the coast. They have replaced the mangroves with rice paddies, fields of palm trees, and shrimp farms.

Over the last 50 years, about a third of the world's mangroves have been lost. Some types of mangroves have been hit so hard that 11 species are likely to be **extinct** soon.

As many as 97 square miles (251 sq km) of mangrove forests are lost every year. That's an area twice the size of San Francisco, California!

Protecting Our Protectors

Around the world, people have begun to realize how important mangroves are to all living things. Governments are now enforcing laws that make it illegal to remove mangroves when building along the coastline. Some former mangrove forests that were replaced by farms are being restored. And environmental groups are busy planting young mangroves in coastal mudflats to create new forests.

Mangroves are always working to protect the lives of plants and animals within their ecosystems, and now help is on the way to protect the mangroves.

Scientists are studying the best ways to bring mangroves back. Some researchers have found that a certain kind of young mangroves survive best if their roots stay above water for two-thirds of the day.

Save the Mangroves

Because mangroves are so important to the health and well-being of life on our planet, when they are in danger, we all are. Luckily, there are some easy things we can do to protect this keystone species.

Learn more about mangroves, and teach your friends and family how they are a keystone species.

Keep pollution out of the waters where mangroves live. Do not pour any chemicals down your drain or in your gutters. What goes down your drain often ends up in the water.

Cut down on your use of heat-trapping fuel by biking, walking, or using public transportation whenever possible.

Join coastline cleanup days.

Join, donate to, or volunteer for mangrove protection and conservation programs.

Glossary

algae plantlike living things often found in water

carbon dioxide a greenhouse gas given off when fossil fuels are burned

climate the usual, expected weather in a place

ecosystems communities of animals and plants that depend on one another

estuaries places where ocean tides meet river currents

extinct gone, having died out completely

filter to remove unwanted materials by passing them through something

fossil fuels energy sources made from the remains of plants and animals that died millions of years ago

glands parts of living things that do a specific job

habitat a place in nature where plants and animals live

nutrients substances needed by living things for health and growth

pollutants things that make environments unclean and unhealthy

predators animals that hunt and eat other animals

sediment tiny pieces of rock that are carried by moving water

species groups that plants and animals are divided into, according to similar characteristics

toxins poisons that can cause harm to plants and animals

Read More

Bergin, Raymond. *Wetland Life Connections (Life on Earth! Biodiversity Explained).* Minneapolis: Bearport Publishing Company, 2023.

Levy, Janey. *Mangroves Grow in Salt Water! (World's Weirdest Plants).* New York: Gareth Stevens Publishing, 2020.

Rothery, Ben. *Ocean Planet: Animals of the Sea and Shore.* New York: Tilbury House Publishers, 2021.

Learn More Online

1. Go to **www.factsurfer.com** or scan the QR code below.

2. Enter "**Keystone Mangrove Trees**" into the search box.

3. Click on the cover of this book to see a list of websites.

Index

About the Author

Olivia was born and raised in Massachusetts but now calls the city of Philadelphia her home. She is a preschool teacher and museum educator. While Olivia has never seen a mangrove tree in real life, she hopes to one day visit this amazing keystone species!